THE EARLY YEARS OF
LONDON DIESELS

MICHAEL WELCH

Capital Transport

CONTENTS

First published 2002

ISBN 185414 253 4

Published by Capital Transport Publishing,
38 Long Elmes, Harrow Weald, Middlesex

Printed by CS Graphics, Singapore

Front cover In this splendidly evocative portrait of the interior of the South Eastern part of Victoria station (known to railwaymen as the 'Chatham Side'), a BRCW Type 3 is seen at the buffer stops after arrival with the empty stock of the 'Night Ferry' from Stewarts Lane depot. The locomotive depicted is No. D6544 and this picture was taken in January 1963. The long-established 'Night Ferry' was a prestigious international express which conveyed continental Wagon-Lits sleeping-cars and provided a through service for sleeping-car passengers from London to Paris and Brussels via Dover and Dunkerque. This train also offered ordinary seating accommodation, but these coaches did not run through to the continent. In the late 1950s the train left Victoria at 10.0pm and the advertised arrival time in Paris was 9.0am the following morning, and at that time the first class return fare for travel in a single berth compartment was £22 11*s*. 0*d*. The 'Night Ferry' was a remarkable survivor from the romantic age of rail travel but was expensive to operate, and increasing competition from the airlines led to its withdrawal in October 1980. *John Snell*

Back cover Hauling a down empty train of suburban carriages, Brush Type 2 A1A-A1A No D5609, in quite presentable external condition, climbs past Holloway in August 1962. Note the vehicle immediately behind the locomotive, which is one of a small batch of 28 non-corridor second open coaches constructed at Doncaster Works for Eastern Region outer suburban services operating from King's Cross and Fenchurch Street. These 57-feet long carriages consisted of two identical saloons with four seating bays connected by a small passageway in the centre of the coach. The passage gave access to two toilets, one on each side of the passageway. These vehicles were known to BR staff as 'Second Lavatory Open' coaches, or SLOs. The next coach in the formation is a Brake Second (BS) which comprised of six second class passenger compartments and a sizeable guard's brake and luggage compartment. These coaches, and the slightly longer seven-compartment version, were much more numerous than the SLOs and could be seen on all BR regions. The origin of the third carriage is given away by its white oval toilet window, a distinguishing feature of the era when Edward Thompson was the LNER's Chief Mechanical Engineer in the 1940s, while the fourth vehicle is a Composite Lavatory (CL) coach – yet another variant of BR Standard suburban carriage. Note the allotments on the right of the shot; one wonders how many of the tenants were railway enthusiasts who combined their railway and gardening interests! *John Snell*

Overleaf To mark the Golden Jubilee of the Institution of Locomotive Engineers, the British Transport Commission arranged an exhibition of locomotives and rolling stock at Marylebone parcels depot on 11th–14th May 1961. A small number of steam locomotives was on display, but the emphasis was very much on modern traction with a creditable variety of types on show. These included the experimental English Electric 2,700hp gas turbine locomotive No. GT3, a couple of diesel hydraulic locomotives from the WR, an SR 2,500hp electric locomotive and a 25kv electric locomotive from the LMR. In addition, there was a selection of both LTE and BR rolling stock. Diesel-electric traction was represented by a 'Deltic', BR/Sulzer 2,500hp Type 4, Brush 1,365hp Type 2, SR 1,500hp BRCW Type 3 and rather strangely perhaps, one of the unsuccessful NBL Type 1 800hp Bo-Bos. Undoubtedly the star of the show for diesel fans was the 'Deltic' and in this picture a queue of eager enthusiasts is seen awaiting their turn to enter the cab of No. D9003, which was later named *Meld*. The BR/Sulzer Type 4 No. D28, on the right, does not seem to be attracting quite as much attention. *Neil Davenport*

INTRODUCTION

It is a startling fact that when BR's Modernisation Plan was announced in 1955 only seven main line diesel locomotives were in operation on the system, and of the four pre-nationalisation companies only the LMSR and Southern Railway had taken any practical steps to build main line locomotives. This policy of relying on the steam locomotive had been continued by the Chief Mechanical Engineer of the newly formed British Railways, who introduced a series of BR Standard steam locomotives.

When the Modernisation Plan was approved, dieselisation was seen as a vital aspect of BR's 'new look', as it was considered that the steam locomotive was not capable of further development. Diesel traction offered higher thermal efficiency, better availability and, most of all, improved train speeds in an increasingly competitive transport market. In view of BR's clear lack of experience with main line diesel traction a cautious approach was wisely adopted towards dieselisation, and orders for 174 'pilot scheme' locomotives were placed covering three power groups ranging from 800hp to 2,000hp. Most of these designs incorporated electric transmission, but the Western Region followed the Great Western Railway's long-standing independent tradition and opted for hydraulic transmission instead. Many of BR's most prestigious and high-profile services radiated from London and were therefore earmarked for early dieselisation, the first English Electric Type 4 appearing on the Liverpool Street to Norwich route as early as March 1958, and a few months later diesels became a regular sight at Paddington on West of England expresses. On the freight side, BR's first diesel depot was opened at Devon's Road, Bow, where a fleet of English Electric Type 1s was based.

While the 'pilot scheme' designs were slowly coming off the production lines a review of progress was taking place behind the scenes against a background of BR suffering considerable loss of both passenger and freight traffic. It was decided that the pace of dieselisation needed to be stepped up and additional orders were placed for 'pilot scheme' types, while other untried and untested designs were ordered straight off the drawing board. By the middle of 1959 a total of 684 locomotives was reported to be on order, and this figure, of course, excluded locomotives already delivered to BR. This total included 22 'Deltic' Type 5s, which at that time were scheduled to be numbered D1000-D1021, 147 BR/Sulzer 'Peak' Type 4s, 63 'Warship' Type 4s and 94 BR/Sulzer Type 2s. In addition, 65 BRCW/Sulzer Type 3 'Cromptons' were also on order for the Southern Region, these being BR's first diesel locomotives to be built with electric train heating. It is interesting to note that of the locomotives on order each different class was to work regularly in the Capital at some stage during its life. Some classes were destined to spend only a relatively brief period working in London and were soon moved after a policy change was made in favour of concentrating classes in certain areas to ease maintenance problems. In contrast, the SR 'Cromptons' could still be seen in London in small numbers nearly 40 years after their introduction.

The unpredictable performance of many of the early diesels was sometimes featured in the national press, most of which took a delight in sniping at BR at every opportunity. The press had a field day when, on 11th January 1961, Brush Type 2 No. D5667 failed at Audley End when working the down 'Fenman' from Liverpool Street to King's Lynn. In normal circumstances such an event would not have merited widespread attention but, most unfortunately from BR's point of view, the train was conveying HM the Queen, who was travelling in a special saloon. The train suffered a 56min delay while a stand-by steam locomotive was obtained from Cambridge. The defect which caused the problem was the failure of the Type 2's lubricating pump, apparently the first such failure ever encountered on any ER Brush diesel. It appears that this incident was simply extremely bad luck for BR, but this did not prevent at least one national daily newspaper from running the story on its front page!

The diesels that served London had greatly varying careers and some types, as previously noted, soon left the scene. The English Electric Type 4s, which dominated main line services from Euston in the early 1960s, were largely ousted by electric traction in April 1966. The 'Westerns', the stylish external appearance of which was influenced by the British Transport Commission (BTC) Design Panel, were arguably the most attractive of any of the main line types, but their fate was sealed when their hydraulic transmission was deemed to be non-standard. The final examples of this extremely popular class worked a commemorative tour from Paddington in early 1977. Perhaps the most impressive of all were the superb 'Deltics', an everyday sight on expresses from King's Cross for more than 20 years, until they were mostly displaced by High Speed Trains. The famous 'Deltic' type attained celebrity status when ITN television cameras were present for the arrival at King's Cross of the last official 'Deltic'-hauled train, and the class's demise in ordinary service was featured on a Saturday night television news bulletin! Some aspects of the dieselisation policy in the 1950s/60s could certainly have been better handled, but at least the proliferation of different locomotive types produced a most interesting scene for the enthusiast, in sad contrast to the dull uniformity of today when locomotive-hauled passenger trains are such a rarity. Looking back at events which occurred when the modernisation scheme was in full swing, perhaps the most extraordinary aspect of the dieselisation programme was that BR was still building steam engines at the same time as they were ordering hundreds of diesels which were intended to replace them!

While compiling this album I have, once again, received unfailing assistance from many accomplished photographers up and down the country, to whom I offer grateful thanks. I have endeavoured to produce a balanced selection of pictures but, almost needless to say, some lines are much better covered than others. The Midland Line from St Pancras never attracted photographers in steam days and the same is true of the later years. I would, for example, have liked to include a colour shot of one of the elusive Metrovick Co-Bos in London, but none seem to exist. I am fortunate to have had assistance from Bob Dalton, Chris Evans and David J. Fakes to whom I am most grateful. They have scrutinised the original manuscript and suggested many improvements which have considerably enhanced the end result. I accept responsibility for any errors which have remained undetected.

Michael Welch
Burgess Hill
West Sussex
January 2002

WESTERN REGION LINES

In this attractive scene 'Western' Class No. D1001 *Western Pathfinder* sits at the buffer stops at Paddington station's Platform Nine following arrival with a train from Birmingham Snow Hill on a January evening in 1963. Unfortunately, few photographers experimented with night-time shots which could often be very rewarding, and in this case the photographer has produced a particularly evocative picture despite the presence of wicker baskets and piles of mail bags. No. D1001 was one of the examples constructed at Swindon Works, from where it emerged in February 1962, painted experimentally in maroon livery. Other locomotives were turned out in golden ochre, desert sand and green livery. Maroon was eventually adopted as the standard colour for the class, with small yellow warning panels which gave way to blue livery with full yellow warning ends from around 1967. *John Snell*

A general view of the splendid interior of Paddington station, taken in the mid-1960s, showing one of the Western Region's 'Blue Pullman' units waiting at Platform Five. The concept of these luxury trains was created during the 1955 Modernisation Plan, when the British Transport Commission decided to introduce semi-streamlined diesel trains between important business centres in order to combat the threat from the motorway network which was being planned. Three eight-car sets were constructed for the WR by Metropolitan Cammell & Co. at their Birmingham works and these commenced trials in early 1960. Two six-car sets for the LMR were built at the same time. The units were powered by two 12 cylinder 1,000hp NBL/MAN diesel engines which were located in the driving motor coaches of each unit. The sets were extremely well appointed, perhaps the most novel feature being the air conditioning, this being the first time this equipment was fitted to a production train in Great Britain. In addition, the stock had inward-opening doors of traditional Pullman design and double glazing was fitted throughout. Small narrow strip venetian blinds were provided between the two panes of glass, these being operated by small handles by the sides of the windows. Another Pullman feature was the press buttons below each window which enabled passengers to summon the attendant. Unfortunately, the units suffered from bad riding which was a source of complaint and this problem was never satisfactorily resolved. The WR sets entered traffic in September 1960 on the Bristol to Paddington and Wolverhampton–Birmingham–Paddington routes. In each case the units formed a morning business service to the Capital and were then booked for a mid-day 'fill-in' turn on the same routes before working an evening return business service. Occasionally, the units strayed away from their usual haunts, one case being on 20th March 1964 when a WR set formed a Swansea to Aintree Grand National race special. In many respects the Pullman units were very successful, but by the early 1970s much of their equipment was obsolete and, being such a tiny fleet, they were becoming increasingly expensive to maintain. In late 1972 the British Railways Board announced that the 'Blue Pullmans' would be withdrawn from the summer 1973 timetable. Efforts were made to sell the sets to an overseas railway administration, and several attempts were made to preserve at least one of the cars. Neither met with any success, however, and all of the vehicles were subsequently scrapped. *John Edgington*

The reflections on the wet platform and glow from the cosy cab of the locomotive enhance the indefinable magic of the railway at night. Here, 'Hymek' Type 3 B-B No. D7063 awaits departure from Paddington with a Cheltenham train in January 1963. The first 'Hymek' was completed in April 1961 at Beyer Peacock's Gorton Works, Manchester, and the fleet eventually totalled 101 examples. The locomotives, which weighed 74 tons, were powered by a 1,700hp Maybach MD870 diesel engine and incorporated Mekydro K184U hydro-mechanical transmission. Commonwealth bogies were fitted, and all of the locomotives had steam heating apparatus. The standard livery adopted for the class was Brunswick green with white window surrounds and a light green band at solebar level. Small yellow warning panels were later applied. No. D7063 was only a few weeks old at the time of this photograph and only had a very short working life, being withdrawn in October 1971. It was broken-up at Swindon Works a year later. Note that at least the first two Mk 1 coaches forming the train are equipped with B4 bogies, which were coming into use at that time. *John Snell*

A very dirty 'Hymek' B-B locomotive, No. D7001, brings empty stock into Paddington station in August 1962. Note the chocolate-and-cream liveried buffet restaurant car in the adjacent platform. The external appearance of these locomotives was elegant and uncomplicated, largely as a result of the influence of the BTC's Design Panel which insisted on minimising extraneous detail. The class was primarily intended to replace mixed-traffic 4–6–0 steam locomotives and as a result they ranged far and wide on the WR, although they were never a common sight in the West Country. Their passenger duties often took them onto the Southern Region, while freight workings included regular sorties to LMR and ER yards in the London area. Some members of the class survived in traffic for less than eight years, but No. D7001 lived to be one of the longest-serving examples. It entered service at Bristol in July 1961 and remained active until March 1974, its final shed being Old Oak Common. Following withdrawal it met its fate at Cohen's, Kettering, scrapyard, unlike most of the class which were scrapped at Swindon. *Geoff Rixon*

A Swansea express is depicted leaving Paddington on 19th August 1963 behind 'Western' Class No. D1042 *Western Princess*. Note that all of the train is in maroon livery, thus presenting a very uniform appearance which purists might argue was more suited to the London Midland Region! Interestingly, *Western Princess* was one of 44 of these machines built on that region, being outshopped by Crewe Works in October 1962. It commenced its brief career stationed at Old Oak Common shed and, like all of the survivors of the class, ended its days at Laira depot, Plymouth, this particular locomotive being condemned in July 1973.
R.C. Riley

Another classic shot of a WR express leaving Paddington behind a diesel hydraulic locomotive, this time showing 'Warship' Class B-B 2,000hp No. D801 *Vanguard* departing in charge of the down 'Torbay Express' on 13th August 1960. This train was booked for diesel haulage from 27th July 1959 when No. D808 *Centaur* powered the down train from London, the honour of working the up service going to sister engine No. D807 *Caradoc*. The introduction of diesel power resulted in the journey time between Paddington and Exeter being reduced to 165min. which, at that time, was the fastest ever between the two cities. No. D801 was finished in green livery, with a grey waistband and polished metal trim, the cast nameplates being positioned in the middle of the bodysides beneath the BR locomotive emblem. In about late 1964 the WR decided to extend the maroon livery adopted for the 'Westerns' to the 'Warship' Class locomotives. This resulted in the disappearance of the bodyside grey stripe and replacement of the locomotive emblem by the roundel normally used on coaching stock. The WR's plans to repaint the fleet were, however, overtaken by the arrival of BR's blue colour scheme just over a year later, so only about half of the 'Warships' actually received maroon livery. Most observers would probably agree that the blue livery was less attractive than either green or maroon colours and certainly suffered as a result of regular 'cleaning'. The strong chemical cleaning fluids used in this process soon knocked the shine off paintwork and after a long period in traffic locomotives' paintwork often looked faded and badly stained, as shown in the photo opposite. *R.C. Riley*

Photographed on a sunny 19th October 1963, 'Hymek' No. D7020 passes Subway Junction at the head of a down parcels train. The train is composed of an incredible assortment of vehicles; formed immediately behind the locomotive appears to be an LMSR-designed bogie full brake van (known to railwaymen as a 'BG'), while a number of four-wheeled vans are also visible. Note the short tunnel in the bottom right corner, through which the tracks of the Metropolitan Hammersmith & City Line pass. *R.C. Riley*

In this view 'Warship' Class No. D800 *Sir Brian Robertson*, the first of the class to be constructed, is depicted speeding past West London Junction (which is just out of sight beyond the bridge) with a Plymouth to Paddington train on 29th September 1962. No. D800 earned its place in history when, on 16th July 1958, it hauled the 1.20pm Penzance to Paddington train, which was the inaugural through run with a diesel hydraulic locomotive. It even carried a special headboard to mark the occasion. This machine was named after the Chairman of the British Transport Commission who apparently (and some experts might say, misguidedly) gave the WR the go-ahead to proceed with the introduction of the diesel hydraulics, reportedly against the wishes of many officials in the BR hierarchy. The glory days of the class were short lived, however, and in the late-1960s as a result of more demanding schedules and falling reliability, the 'Warships' increasingly found themselves relegated to less prestigious duties, including use on freight workings. In addition they were less powerful than either the 'Westerns' or the Brush Type 4s (later Class 47) and this was another factor against them. In later years the class was plagued by problems associated with loss of coolant and control system failures, the batch built by the North British Locomotive Company being especially prone to faults of this type which resulted in locomotives spending weeks at a time out of service awaiting rectification. No. D800 displays a traditional stencil type route indicator and headcode discs, which were originally fitted to the first 14 examples to be built. *Paul Leavens*

A multiplicity of dmu types operated in the London area during the period covered by this album, but sadly it seems that few were photographed in colour. This picture of a Gloucester Railway Carriage & Wagon Co. Motor Parcels Van, or Driving Motor Parcels & Mail Van (DMPMV) as the vehicles were officially known, is an exception to this rule. It shows car No. W55991 speeding towards Paddington at West London Junction, while a GWR-designed pannier tank heads in the direction of Old Oak Common on an adjacent track with a rake of empty main line stock. This picture was taken on 29th September 1962. No. W55991 was one of six cars ordered by the WR for parcels traffic in the London and Birmingham areas and these were delivered in 1959. The cars, which weighed 41 tons, were powered by two horizontally mounted Albion 230hp engines with standard mechanical transmission. In order to increase their usefulness in service the cars were fitted with gangways at both ends and could work in multiple with other parcels cars and dmus, thus enabling parcels to be sorted in transit. Three pairs of sliding doors were fitted on each side, thus giving excellent accessibility. There was a two-digit indicator blind situated under each windscreen, thus enabling a four character headcode to be displayed. The engine exhaust pipes were carried up to the roof level beside the gangway connection at one end of the car. *Paul Leavens*

Photographed in the sub-zero conditions which typified the 1962/63 winter, 'Hymek' B-B No. D7017 is seen near Old Oak Common at the head of a down parcels working on 29th December 1962. No. D7017 entered service at Bristol (Bath Road) depot in January 1962 and finished its short BR career when it was withdrawn from Old Oak Common shed in March 1975. Being one of the very last survivors, it was one of the four members of the class fortunate enough to be selected for private preservation, and at the time of writing can be seen on the West Somerset Railway. *Paul Leavens*

Brush Type 4 2,750hp Co-Co No. D1695 is depicted at Old Oak Common shed on 14th August 1966. The widespread introduction of these machines, combined with the transfer of the English Electric Type 4 Co-Cos (later Class 50) from the LMR, soon eliminated the non-standard diesel hydraulics. Despite its very smart and impressive appearance in two-tone green livery in this illustration, No. D1695 was destined to lead an undistinguished life. It was outshopped by the Brush Locomotive Co. (other examples were constructed at Crewe) in December 1963 and was initially based at Oxley shed in the West Midlands. No. D1695 was renumbered 47 107 under the TOPS scheme in February 1974. It was originally built with a vacuum brake only, but was converted to dual braking at some stage during its career. A steam heating boiler was fitted when new but this was later removed, thus restricting No. D1695's use on passenger workings to the summer season and ensuring that it spent most of its time on mundane freight work. It was taken out of traffic in June 1991. *Frank Hornby*

This everyday mid-1960s scene at Old Oak Common shed shows four mostly unidentified locomotives clustered around a turntable. They are (from left to right) a 'Western' (later Class 52) in maroon livery, a Brush Type 4 (later Class 47), North British Locomotive Co. Type 2 No. D6352 and a 'Hymek' Type 3 all in green livery. The NBL Type 2s and 'Hymeks' were classified 22 and 35 respectively under the five digit TOPS renumbering scheme, but no locomotives from either class ever carried their TOPS numbers. During the late 1960s various pronouncements were made by BR regarding future motive power policy and the writing was clearly on the wall for the WR's hydraulic fleet. At one time BR announced that all of the hydraulics would be phased out by the end of 1973, but this forecast proved to be over optimistic. The last of the NBL Type 2s was condemned in early 1972, but the 'Hymeks' lasted until March 1975. Much to the delight of many diesel enthusiasts, a small number of 'Westerns' carried on until February 1977 and it is probably true to say that the 'Westerns' became one of the most popular diesel classes. *Frank Hornby*

Photographed in the last year of its service, a six-car former Midland Pullman unit sits out in the sunshine at Old Oak Common on 16th July 1972. Both Midland Pullman units were moved to the WR following the abandonment of that service when electric trains were introduced on the West Coast Main Line in April 1966. By the time of this photograph the attractive and very distinctive original blue Pullman livery, which greatly added to the appeal of these trains, had been replaced by the new standard BR colour scheme that had been applied to the Pullmans used on other routes. In the opinion of most observers it was hardly a change for the better. The WR modified the former Midland Pullman units to run in multiple, work which involved the fitting of rather clumsy and very prominent body-mounted jumpers at the front end of each power car. This work was necessary to enable two six-car units to operate in multiple on a Bristol to Paddington morning business service. The units then separated, one forming a train to Oxford and back, while the other did a round trip to Bristol, before they were reunited in the evening to provide a down rush-hour working to Bristol. They were all withdrawn, as previously mentioned in this album, in May 1973. *Frank Hornby*

A North British Type 2 B-B diesel hydraulic locomotive, No. D6345, is the subject of this picture which was taken at Old Oak Common depot in August 1966. Note the spoked wheels, which are most unusual on a diesel locomotive. A total of 58 examples of this class was built by NBL in Glasgow. Apart from the six prototype locomotives which had a slightly different 1,000hp version, the class employed a NBL/MAN L12V18/21B diesel engine which developed 1,100hp. These machines weighed 65 tons and possessed a top speed of 75mph. All of the locomotives were fitted with a train heating boiler. There were other considerable design differences between the prototype locomotives (Nos D6300–5) and the remainder of the class which prevented them from working in multiple. Consequently, the first six locomotives were largely confined to the West Country throughout their lives, but the others travelled widely and were regularly noted on empty coaching stock duties at Paddington. The class was primarily designed for light passenger, branch line and pilot work but, unfortunately, the last member entered service in November 1962, just four months prior to the publication of the Beeching Report which foreshadowed a marked reduction in such duties. Withdrawals commenced in 1968 and the final locomotives left in traffic were condemned in January 1972. *Frank Hornby*

A GWR-designed diesel railcar, No. W31W, is seen at Southall shed on 20th June 1959. The GWR experimented with the internal combustion engine as long ago as 1911, when a solitary petrol-electric four-wheeled railcar (No. 100) was purchased. The railcar employed a 40hp petrol engine that drove a dynamo supplying current to two electric motors. This car worked for a time on the Slough to Windsor branch, which later became a regular haunt of the GWR diesel railcars. Unfortunately, the performance of the railcar did not measure up to the GWR's expectations and in 1919 it was sold to Lever Brothers of Port Sunlight, Cheshire. The GWR did not venture into internal combustion power again until 1933, when a single-engined 121hp streamlined railcar began to operate at Reading. The car proved to be so successful that three further cars, this time with two 121hp engines, were ordered for express services, and these went into traffic on the South Wales to Birmingham route in 1934. Further cars were built during the ensuing years, No. W31W being one of a batch of 15 vehicles ordered in the late 1930s for branch line work and constructed at the GWR's Swindon Works. It had two engines which gave a total of 210hp, provided 48 seats and even had a luggage compartment at one end. The cars in this batch had the extra advantage of being able to run in pairs at busy periods with one or two specially converted locomotive-hauled coaches between them. The GWR diesel railcars were particularly associated with Worcestershire and also the Bristol area, but some saw service in the London area on the Slough to Windsor line, as previously mentioned, and also on the West Drayton to Staines branch. In the mid-1950s a number of the vehicles were destroyed by fire, but No. W31W survived until withdrawn from service at Worcester in August 1962, just a few months before the last of these interesting railcars was condemned. *Trevor Owen*

The road overbridge immediately east of
Southall station, which has been a favourite
vantage point for generations of train
spotters and railway photographers, offers a
clear, uninterrupted view of the Great
Western main line and also of movements
at Southall engine shed, which dominates
the background. The former branch to
Brentford, which lost its passenger service
in May 1942, can be seen on the right of the
picture. This illustration shows a three-car
dmu reversing across the main line towards
Southall station, apparently before forming
a train to Staines. Virtually identical
batches of these units were constructed by
at least two different manufacturers, but
units built by Pressed Steel, which were
introduced in 1959, were the most numerous
on WR routes in the London area and this
unit is almost certainly one of those.
Unfortunately the vehicle number, which
would have positively identified the unit, is
not quite readable. *Cliff Woodhead*

Another picture taken from the same
viewpoint as that in the previous shot,
shows 'Warship' Class A1A-A1A Type 4
No. D601 *Ark Royal* approaching Southall
station with a train from Paddington to the
West of England in 1961. An order for five of
these diesel hydraulic locomotives was
placed by the WR in 1955 as a first step
towards the elimination of steam traction
on the region. The contract was given to the
North British Locomotive Company of
Glasgow and the first locomotive, No. D600
Active, was released for testing in November
1957 and commenced regular operation
during the first half of 1958. It was soon
joined by No. D601 and delivery of the
entire class was completed by January 1959.
These 117-ton machines were powered by
two NBL/MAN 1,000hp engines. During its
brief life the class's principal sphere of
activity was the London to Bristol and
Penzance routes. *Ark Royal* achieved fame
when, on 16th June 1958, it hauled the down
'Cornish Riviera Express' non-stop from
Paddington to Plymouth and even managed
to surmount the formidable Hemerdon Bank
without assistance. Like other hydraulic
classes, the careers of these locomotives
were swiftly terminated when BR decided to
standardise on diesel electric traction, and
all five members of the class were
withdrawn simultaneously in December
1967. None was preserved, despite the fact
that two locomotives survived intact for a
considerable time following withdrawal.
Cliff Woodhead

The Great Western Railway was justly famed for its network of idyllic country branch lines, the vast majority of which fell victim to the misguided Beeching cuts of the 1960s. The GWR even had a few branches in the London area, including two separate lines to Uxbridge, although perhaps it should be mentioned that the Uxbridge High Street to Denham branch was closed as long ago as September 1939. The branch line from West Drayton to Staines West survived for much longer, not losing its passenger service until 29th March 1965. Here, Pressed Steel single unit railcar, No. W55028, is depicted at a rather deserted Staines West station. The WR took delivery of a total of 16 of these vehicles, which were officially known as 'driving motor brake seconds' (DMBS), in 1960. They had 65 second class seats, weighed 37 tons and were powered by two 150hp engines. This scene was recorded on 30th January 1965, the day of Sir Winston Churchill's funeral, hence the flag flying at half-mast. *Hugh Ballantyne*

THE CHILTERN LINE

A Derby-built high-density four-car dmu leaves Marylebone station forming the 1.10pm to Aylesbury on 16th July 1974, by which time these units were approaching the middle of their working lives. The drab BR corporate blue livery does little to enhance the unit's uninspiring appearance. Forty-one of these sets were built in two batches specifically for commuter services from Marylebone to Aylesbury, High Wycombe and Banbury, although six of the second series were allocated to the Liverpool area to work between Liverpool, Warrington and Manchester. The design of this stock was influenced by the BTC's Design Panel and the units offered a high level of comfort. The first class accommodation, for example, consisted of 'three-a-side' seating in an open saloon, and every seat was provided with an individual reading light. Each power car was fitted with two Albion 230hp engines, although these were later downrated to 200hp to prolong the engine life. Note that being suburban units they had doors to each seating bay. These units were phased out in the early 1990s when they were replaced by Class 165 units. *Chris Evans*

THE WEST COAST LINE

A view of the English Electric prototype 2,700hp diesel-electric locomotive No. DP2 at the buffer stops inside Euston station in 1962 after arrival with a train from the north. No. DP2, which entered revenue-earning service on the LMR in May 1962, was externally almost identical to a production series 'Deltic', but contained an English Electric 16CSVT diesel engine similar to that used on the D200 Class Type 4 locomotives. The initials 'DP' were an abbreviation for 'diesel prototype'. It was mounted on bogies which were partly interchangeable with those of the English Electric Type 3 and Type 5 locomotives and had a maximum service speed of 90mph. No. DP2, which was extremely reliable in service, spent its initial period of BR test running on the West Coast Main Line and was reportedly often placed in traffic unaccompanied by any engineering staff, such was the confidence that BR had in the machine. In June 1963 No. DP2 was returned to Vulcan Foundry for attention to its bogies and traction motors and thereafter worked on the East Coast Main Line mostly on 'Deltic' diagrams. During another visit to its manufacturers in May 1965 No. DP2 was repainted in a revised two-tone green livery. In 1966 modifications were carried out on the locomotive, including the fitting of wheelslip control equipment which was tested during trials on the Shap incline, when No. DP2 started a 16-coach train and apparently reached 30mph in 575 yards. Sadly, this distinctive locomotive was damaged beyond repair in a collision near Thirsk in July 1967 and was scrapped during the following year. Many of the design features of No. DP2 were incorporated in the Class 50 locomotives. *Geoff Rixon*

During the 1960s Euston station was completely rebuilt as part of the scheme to modernise the West Coast Main Line, and by the time this picture was taken the 'old Euston' had disappeared and had been replaced by a rather characterless modern building, a small part of which is just visible. The shot depicts English Electric Type 1 1,000hp Bo-Bo diesel locomotive Nos D8006 (nearest to the camera) and D8039 entering the station with (what appears to be) a short test train on 21st April 1966. *John Hayward*

A classic shot of LMSR-designed Co-Co locomotive No. 10000 climbing Camden Bank at the head of the 5.25pm Euston to Northampton train on 4th June 1962. The train appears to be formed entirely of compartment coaches and is being assisted at the rear by another locomotive, a BR/Sulzer Type 2, which had presumably brought the empty stock into Euston. It is most doubtful that No. 10000 really required a banking engine on such a relatively light load and more likely that this was merely the most convenient way of removing the Type 2 from the station area. Soon after the end of the Second World War the LMSR announced that it was keen to investigate the advantages of diesel traction and stated that it was going to construct two prototype locomotives. No. 10000 emerged from Derby Works in November 1947, just before nationalisation of the railways, painted in black with a silver waist-height band, roof and bogies. It carried the letters 'LMS' on the bodysides. The 1,600hp locomotive weighed 121tons 10cwt and had a maximum speed of 93mph. The second of the prototypes, No. 10001, appeared in July 1948. Both engines worked for a time on the LMR, but in March 1953 were moved to the Southern Region where they operated from Nine Elms shed. In early 1955 both locomotives were returned to the LMR. No. 10000 was withdrawn from service in December 1963 following about a year stored unserviceable, while its sister locomotive lasted until March 1966. *John Dewing/Colour-Rail*

An interesting mid-1960s scene just outside Euston station which was photographed from almost the same position as the previous picture. The shot was taken in June 1966, not long after the start of electric services to Liverpool and Manchester during April of that year. Nearest to the camera is English Electric Type 1 Bo-Bo No. D8038 which appears to be 'rescuing' a 'dead' electric locomotive, while a Euston to Watford three-car emu rattles by on an adjacent track. These Type 1 locomotives became one of the most successful and longest serving of the types introduced under the BR Modernisation Plan, the first example appearing as long ago as June 1957. At the time of writing some members of the class, retained by various companies for specialist purposes, can still be seen operating on the national railway network. *John Dewing*

In steam days Camden engine shed, or 'motive power depot' as it was officially known, was a place of pilgrimage for enthusiasts because it housed some of Sir William Stanier's mighty 'Princess Coronation' Class Pacifics which were employed on the West Coast Main Line's most arduous express passenger services. In September 1963, however, Camden shed was closed to steam traction and its few surviving steam engines were moved to Willesden. The rather makeshift and ramshackle premises are seen here in this view which was taken in March 1966. Unfortunately, one of the crucial mistakes made by BR in the early years of the dieselisation programme concerned the lack of provision of proper maintenance facilities for the diesel fleet, many of which were maintained in unsuitable conditions, sometimes side by side with steam engines. The locomotive seen here nearest to the camera is No. D306 which, many years later, achieved fame as the final surviving member of its class in green livery. Much to the delight of the enthusiast fraternity it was repainted green during a classified repair in 1978, despite the corporate image blue livery which was usually rigidly adhered to at the time. Consequently, No. 40 106 (as No. D306 had become) gained celebrity status and was rescued for preservation following its withdrawal in April 1983. No. D307 was not so lucky, being withdrawn in December 1981 and later cut-up at Crewe Works. *John Dewing*

Viewed from the roof of Camden motive power depot, English Electric 1Co-Co1 2,000hp Type 4 No. D342 is seen powering an unidentified semi-fast train from Euston on 18th September 1963. Trains starting from Euston were immediately faced with the formidable 1 in 68 to 1 in 77 gradients of Camden bank and in steam days most heavy trains were given banking assistance during the initial stage of the climb. This was a legacy of the decision by the London & Birmingham Railway to change their original plan to build a terminus at Camden Town, and opt instead for a station nearer to the centre of London at Euston Grove. The extension had to cross the Regent's Canal which resulted in the severe incline to be negotiated by trains leaving Euston. *John Dewing*

Another panoramic shot taken from a high vantage point at Camden, this time from a position on the coaling tower. It depicts an unidentified English Electric 2,000hp locomotive passing Primrose Hill station with the up 'Ulster Express' on 28th October 1962. Note the electrified suburban tracks in the foreground which are used by services from Euston to Watford. These trains could not therefore call at Primrose Hill station which was latterly served by Broad Street to Watford trains during the rush hours only. The girder bridge carries Regents Park Road across the railway. Some of the rooftops of the elegant Victorian villas which are typical of this affluent area of north London can be seen on the horizon. It is said that the closure of Camden shed was hastened by complaints about smoke from nearby residents. Surely the magical aroma of steam locomotive smoke was preferable to diesel fumes, especially if came from a 'Duchess' Pacific! *John Dewing*

During the first half of the 1960s services along the southern section of the West Coast Main Line were severely curtailed due to electrification work, and those that did operate were frequently held up by engineering possessions of the kind depicted in this picture of Type 4 No. D372 heading the Sunday 2pm Euston to Liverpool train past Kensal Green on 4th October 1964. On some occasions, when incidents occurred, the delays were of nightmare proportions, especially when operational flexibility was restricted by running lines being out of use. Many passengers from London to Manchester used the enhanced service which ran from St Pancras, while Birmingham and Wolverhampton passengers were encouraged to use trains from Paddington, from where additional services were also provided. *Hugh Ballantyne*

English Electric Type 1 No. D8044 approaches the west end of Kensal Green tunnel with a Willesden to Stratford transfer freight on 4th August 1962. Its train appears to be formed entirely of short wheelbase vans, known to railwaymen as 'vanfits', which were unsuited to high-speed operation and have long since disappeared from the scene. There are six running lines at this point, the fast tracks being in the foreground, while the electrified suburban lines are behind the train. Constructed at Vulcan Foundry in November 1959, No. D8044 remained in service until September 1989, its final shed being Toton. *Paul Leavens*

A general view of Willesden traction maintenance depot on 14th August 1966 showing English Electric Type 4 No. D370 standing in the yard accompanied by a LMR Western Lines a.c. four-car suburban emu. These units were introduced in the early 1960s for use on the newly electrified routes from Manchester and Liverpool to Crewe and were later used more widely as electrification was extended southwards. Inside the depot, the front end of a Euston to Watford d.c. emu can be seen together with an electric locomotive and 350hp diesel shunter. This depot is still very much in use today, servicing traction employed on the West Coast Main Line. *Frank Hornby*

'Oh dear, what should we do next?', might very well have been the reaction of the Willesden shed staff seen here following the derailment of diesel shunter No. 12074 in a shunting mishap on 25th October 1959. Sister engine No. 12075 – luckily still very much on the rails – is nearest to the camera. Note that the cab end panelling is painted plain black which hardly makes the locomotive visible to staff working on the track. These 350hp 0–6–0 locomotives were designed by the LMSR and the first members of the type appeared in 1945. They had English Electric engines, weighed 47½ tons and had two nose-suspended traction motors, unlike a previous LMSR design which had a single motor and incorporated a jackshaft drive. Examples remained at work on the national system until the early 1970s. 25th October 1959 may not have been the high point of No. 12074's career, but it later had a marked change of fortune when it became one of a number of these locomotives to survive into preservation. *Trevor Owen*

No. 10201, seen here in the roundhouse at Willesden shed on 25th March 1961, was the first of three 1Co-Co1 locomotives built by the Southern Region, which made its initial move towards diesel traction in the early 1950s. No. 10201, which was completed at Ashford Works in November 1950, had a 1,600hp sixteen cylinder English Electric engine, weighed 135 tons and possessed a top speed of 90mph. The machine was painted in main line black and silver livery. It underwent testing on the SR for a brief period before moving to the LMR in January 1951 for trial running between St. Pancras and Derby. After returning to the SR No. 10201 was displayed at the Festival of Britain exhibition. Its sister engine No. 10202 was completed in July 1951 and in October of the same year both locomotives, which were based at Nine Elms shed, commenced regular operation on Waterloo to West of England trains. Both machines were occasionally taken out of service for attention and modification work at Brighton Works. In March 1954 a third locomotive, No. 10203, was completed, but unlike its sisters it was constructed at Brighton Works. No. 10203 incorporated considerable design differences to the earlier machines, most notably its 2,000hp engine and marginally reduced weight. For a short time all three engines worked together on the Western Section of the SR, but by mid-1955 they had all been transferred to Camden where they worked alongside Nos 10000 and 10001. Nos 10201 and 10202 were sometimes employed on the 'Royal Scot', normally working in tandem as they were not fitted for multiple operation. Being a more powerful machine No. 10203 was generally used separately, and could be found on mundane Euston to Bletchley outer suburban services, in addition to making long distance trips to Manchester and Glasgow. In the late 1950s the locomotives saw little regular use and all were eventually withdrawn in 1963 and later broken-up for scrap. *Trevor Owen*

A portrait of two English Electric 2,000hp 1Co-Co1 Type 4 locomotives at Willesden shed on 20th September 1959, showing No. D223, nearest to the camera, and No. D220. The former was named *Lancastria* in May 1961, while the latter was bestowed with the name *Franconia* in February 1963. Both locomotives were built at Vulcan Foundry and lasted in traffic until the early 1980s. It cannot be denied that these locomotives were amongst the more successful types introduced under the modernisation plan, being based on the Southern Region English Electric Bulleid trio Nos 10201–3. Indeed the class had the same 16SVT engine as No. 10203, itself a 2,000hp development of the 1,600hp version employed on Nos 10201/2. In everyday service it was the temperamental train heating boilers, not engine defects, that were a constant cause of failures, although in later years bogie fractures increased owing to the class's use in tightly-curved sidings. These Type 4s were solid, workmanlike machines which certainly earned their keep on the West Coast Main Line in the days prior to electrification. They were, however, not powerful locomotives bearing in mind their 133-ton weight, particularly when compared to traction working on the West Coast route today. *Frank Hornby*

During the early years of the modernisation plan, steam, diesel and electric traction sometimes worked side-by-side and much of the infrastructure, plus many of the practices of the steam age remained. The vast majority of diesel classes used on passenger trains were fitted with train heating boilers, and perhaps one of the oddest sights was that of a diesel locomotive picking up water for its boiler from water troughs. In this illustration English Electric Type 4 No. D213 (later named *Andania*), hauling the up 'Mancunian', is seen making a splash, so to speak, on Bushey troughs in May 1960. Train heating boilers proved to be one of the most troublesome pieces of equipment used on the new diesel fleets, and were frequently frozen up during frosty weather, just when they were most needed! *Trevor Owen/Colour-Rail*

HARROW & WEALDSTONE TO BELMONT

This vintage view, taken at Harrow & Wealdstone station on 11th April 1954, shows one of the British United Traction Co. experimental 3-car diesel units which were constructed in 1952. It was most likely working the branch service to Belmont when this picture was taken. Eleven of these four-wheeled vehicles were built, four Driving Motor Brake Thirds, three Driving Motor Thirds and four Trailer Thirds. All of the coaches were 37ft 6ins long and the motor coaches were fitted with an AEC 125hp engine with a standard mechanical transmission. The vehicle nearest to the camera is No. M79742, a Driving Motor Brake Third, which weighed a mere 15 tons, and had a small driving compartment at each end plus a guard's van, and provided 28 Third Class seats. This small, self-contained vehicle could, therefore, be used as a railbus on lightly trafficked lines, or as part of a two-car or three-car unit, as seen here. The other coaches in the picture appear to be a Trailer Third (48 seats) in the middle of the train, and a Driving Motor Third (34 seats) at the far end. *Neil Davenport*

The short branch from Harrow & Wealdstone to Stanmore village was opened by the Harrow & Stanmore Railway Company on 25th June 1886 and its opening prompted much residential development around the terminus. In the 1930s further house building occurred in the area, but Stanmore was more conveniently served by the Underground network, which provided an intensive service, and consequently the Harrow to Stanmore branch withered. The section beyond Belmont was closed from 15th September 1952 and the branch was shut completely from 5th October 1964. The last trains ran two days before this date and this view depicts a Park Royal two-car dmu, formed of vehicle Nos M50413 and M56169, waiting to leave Belmont with the 11.20am train to Harrow & Wealdstone. *Hugh Ballantyne*

The charming little station depicted here in this mid-1950s portrait is St Albans Abbey and this shot shows one of the British United Traction Co. experimental units, which was presumably forming a train to Watford. Note the unconventional two-tone grey livery, separated by a red band underneath the windows. Later the livery of these units was changed to green with cream-coloured lining. Initially the units were fitted with skirts, but these were later removed. In 1961 a number of these vehicles were reportedly dumped out of service at Derby Friargate station, so presumably they had ceased passenger operation by that time. *Neil Davenport*

THE MIDLAND LINE

Two six-car Midland Pullman sets were constructed by Metropolitan Cammell, the same firm that built the WR units. The first set reportedly made its debut at St Pancras on trial on 16th November 1959 and the sets entered passenger service on 4th July 1960. Initially, there was only one diagram for the units, which formed a morning businessmen's express from Manchester Central to St Pancras via the Peak route and return evening working. The Midland Pullman immediately gained the title of 'Britain's fastest train', due to its extremely fast timings between St Pancras and Leicester. Prior to their introduction in regular service there was a dispute between the British Transport Commission and the trade unions, who insisted that the cars should be manned by BTC Hotels & Catering Services staff and not those of the Pullman Car Co. which they regarded as a private enterprise company. In 1961 this caused the temporary abandonment of a mid-day St Pancras to Nottingham Midland and return service which the LMR introduced to improve the utilisation of the sets. The Midland Pullman was also dogged by poor riding which at times resulted in a ticklish exercise in dexterity during the service of morning coffee! The sets only lasted on the Midland route until April 1966, when electric working was introduced on the West Coast Main Line between London and Manchester. The latter route offered a much faster Pullman service between the two cities which rendered the diesel Pullman units superfluous, and they subsequently ended their days on the Western Region. This shot was taken at St Pancras station in the early 1960s. *John Edgington*

The Midland route from London rarely seemed to attract photographers, and certainly operations at St Pancras must be the least recorded of any London main line terminal station. Perhaps the fact that it was comparatively quiet and also had a dark, cavernous interior, deterred photographers. In contrast, the station's magnificent exterior was probably the *most* photographed! This picture of shiny BR/Sulzer 1Co-Co1 Type 4 No. D114 waiting to leave on 31st August 1961 with the down 'The Robin Hood' express to Nottingham Midland was the only one of this class in green livery submitted for inclusion in this album. The locomotive looks as though it was brand new when this shot was taken, and indeed it was, being officially released from Crewe Works during period ending 9th September 1961! Perhaps this was its first run, who knows? No. D114, which at the time of this picture was allocated to Derby shed, became No. 45 066 under the TOPS number scheme in February 1975 and remained in ordinary service until July 1987. It then took on a new lease of life in departmental service as No. 97 413 and was eventually cut-up by MC Metals, Glasgow, in December 1991. *Cliff Woodhead*

Another view of a 'Peak' at St Pancras, but in contrast the locomotive is in the much less attractive rail blue livery with full yellow ends, and also has a split route indicator box. This shot of No. 75 awaiting departure at the head of a Sheffield train was taken on 25th October 1969, by which time BR had dispensed with the prefix 'D' denoting diesel traction. This indication was no longer needed owing to the complete withdrawal of standard gauge steam motive power during 1968. Note the wisps of steam by No. 75's front buffer beam, indicating that its train heating boiler was in use. These machines were associated with the Midland Main Line for many years, but their appearances were noticeably reduced following the introduction of High Speed Train sets on the route in the early 1980s. No. 75 survived to become one of the final active members of the class, not being withdrawn until August 1988. *John Spencer Gilks*

Apparently viewed from a lineside allotment, with a patch of blackcurrant bushes in the foreground, Type 2 1,250hp Bo-Bo No. D5384 is seen on a freight working at West Hampstead Midland on 4th May 1963. Note the splendid lower quadrant semaphore signals which are of Midland Railway design. No. D5384 was one of a batch of 37 of these locomotives allocated to Cricklewood for use on Midland Main Line duties in the London area. These were constructed by the Birmingham Railway Carriage & Wagon Co. at Smethwick, and this particular example was outshopped in May 1962. In common with the rest of the class, No. D5384 later moved to Scotland and it was renumbered 27 035. It was destined to have a short working life, being withdrawn as early as September 1976, whereas most members of the class lasted well into the 1980s. It was broken-up at BR's Glasgow Locomotive Works in March 1977. *John Dewing*

During the mid-1960s it became known that a prototype 4,000hp Co-Co diesel-electric locomotive was being built at the Brush Locomotive Works at Loughborough. Numbered HS 4000 and named *Kestrel*, it was handed over to BR for trials, at Marylebone in January 1968. The initials 'HS' stand for Hawker Siddeley. In service its performance was impressive, one of its regular duties being haulage of a Shirebrook to March coal train which was loaded to 1,600 tons. During tests in May 1968 it reportedly took a 665-ton train over Shap, surmounting the summit at 46mph. Brush were keen to see *Kestrel* at the head of a passenger train, but BR engineers were adamant that its axle loading was excessive and Brush agreed to re-bogieing with modified Class 47 bogies. In 1969 it started crew training on the East Coast Main Line and in October commenced regular operation on a King's Cross to Newcastle diagram. In June 1970 *Kestrel* was called in for overhaul and whilst out of traffic negotiations between Brush and the USSR Railways resulted in its sale to the Soviet Union. It briefly returned to service on BR, but was shipped to Russia from Cardiff docks during the spring of 1971. *Kestrel* is depicted on display at Cricklewood in 1969 with an LMR a.c. lines electric locomotive. *D. Rollins/Colour-Rail*

The sun appears to have popped out from behind the clouds just at the right moment for the photographer as BRCW/Sulzer Type 3 Bo-Bo No. 33 021 passes Elstree with a return Uckfield to Flitwick advertised excursion on 31st July 1974. The train is formed of a smartly turned out SR Oxted Line 8-set of air-braked Mk.1 coaches that were still used on some Central Division peak-hour services at that time. At first sight, Flitwick might seem to be a rather obscure destination for a day trip, but Woburn Abbey is close by, so perhaps that was the attraction for most of the participants. *Chris Evans*

Newly-constructed Brush Type 4 Co-Co locomotive No. D1518 awaits departure from King's Cross station with an unidentified express for the north on 22nd June 1963. At the time of this photograph No. D1518 was only a few weeks old, having been outshopped during the previous month. Steam traction had been officially eliminated from the southern end of the East Coast Main Line from 17th June and King's Cross shed closed, but in reality availability of the diesel fleet was poor and steam substitutions continued for many months afterwards. No. D1518 became 47 419 under the TOPS renumbering scheme and lasted until February 1987. *Frank Hornby*

THE EAST COAST LINE

In the early 1960s BR had a need for a six-axle diesel locomotive of at least 2,500hp plus 250hp for electric train heating. In response to this requirement Associated Electrical Industries Ltd, the Birmingham Railway Carriage & Wagon Co. and Sulzer Bros. formed a consortium to design and build a suitable locomotive as a private venture. The outcome of this enterprise was the construction of the 114-ton No. D0260 *Lion* which was inspected by officials of the British Transport Commission at Marylebone on 28th May 1962. It was powered by a Sulzer 12LDA28-C 2,750hp engine and at the time *Lion* was claimed to be the most powerful rail traction single diesel engine in Western Europe with a top speed of 100mph. *Lion*, which was painted in a startling white livery with gold lining, is seen at King's Cross in September 1963. *R. Hill/Colour-Rail*

English Electric Type 2 Bo-Bo No. D5907, commonly known as a 'Baby Deltic', enters King's Cross with an unidentified working, most likely empty coaching stock, on 1st June 1967. 'Ill-fated' might be the most apt description for this class, which was without doubt one of the shortest-lived and least successful classes introduced under the BR modernisation plan. The class employed a Napier Deltic T9–29 1,100hp power unit and possessed a top speed of 75mph. The class seemed to be doomed from the start because the first locomotive to be finished weighed three tons more than the specification, and the makers were forced to undertake various modifications to save weight. These included the replacement of internal steel doors by glass fibre and exchanging other steel components with alloy. It had been intended to employ the class on cross-London freights to the SR between peak-hour suburban passenger work from King's Cross, but even after substantial weight reductions had been achieved the SR still refused to accept them. By June 1959 all ten locomotives had entered service at Hornsey depot, but various engine problems soon developed and by the end of 1959 several power units had been replaced and the class's chronic unreliability was becoming a major headache for the operating authorities and maintenance staff alike. From late 1961 some locomotives were stored unserviceable and those that remained in traffic were confined to local freight duties and e.c.s. workings in the King's Cross area. In 1963 BR agreed terms with English Electric for the total refurbishment of the class and the first 'rebuilt' machine returned to BR in June 1964. The entire class was similarly dealt with and performance improved, but the class was still plagued by problems, including engine room oil leaks and corrosion in the cooling system. BR's national traction plan of the late 1960s pronounced the death sentence on many non-standard, small diesel classes, including these disastrous Type 2s, the last one of which survived in normal service until the early 1970s. *John Hayward*

A Cravens-designed two-car diesel multiple unit bound for Hertford North bounces out of King's Cross on 1st June 1967. Two of Gasworks Tunnel's three grimy portals are visible in the background. Units of this type were an everyday sight at King's Cross from the late-1950s, when they displaced steam traction, until the mid-1970s when the units were phased out due to electrification of the King's Cross suburban lines. *John Hayward*

One can only imagine the deafening sound being produced by English Electric Type 4 1Co-Co1 No. D279 as it strains to pull the 11.0am King's Cross to Edinburgh train up the 1 in 107 gradient near Belle Isle, just beyond Gasworks Tunnel, on 18th March 1961. In the background a 350hp diesel shunter, on shunting duties at King's Cross goods yard, can just be discerned. No. D279 was delivered new to Gateshead in June 1960 and gave nearly 25 years service, being withdrawn from Longsight depot (Manchester) in January 1985 when all of the survivors of this long-lived and much-loved class were condemned, apart from No. D200 (40 122). No. D279 was broken-up with almost indecent haste at Doncaster Works during the month following its withdrawal – a sad end to such a loyal workhorse. *R.C. Riley*

A 'Baby Deltic' at its zenith! Photographed at almost the same location as the previous picture, the 10.30am King's Cross to Cambridge train is seen between Gasworks and Copenhagen tunnels, also on 18th March 1961. English Electric Type 2 Bo-Bo No. D5906 provides the motive power. At this time the multitude of design problems associated with this class were already manifesting themselves, so it is perhaps surprising that No. D5906 was entrusted with a passenger train. Note the varied collection of coaches forming the train, which consists of both compartment and saloon-type Gresley carriages, a Thompson-designed vehicle, which is distinguished by its oval-shaped white toilet windows, and a couple of BR Standard coaches towards the rear. It is interesting to compare this shot with the photograph of sister engine No. D5907, illustrated on page 36. The appearance of No. D5906, in original condition, is quite different to the 'rebuilt' No. D5907, which is sporting a modified livery and four-character train reporting number panel. *R.C.Riley*

A 'Deltic' in its two-tone green livery as most railway enthusiasts will probably prefer to remember them; how impressive and powerful they looked in these colours compared to the uninspiring rail blue which was later applied. In this illustration, photographed on a rather dull and misty 4th October 1964, No. D9017 *The Durham Light Infantry* roars up the bank past Holloway South Down signal box with the 9.40am King's Cross to Harrogate 'The Harrogate Sunday Pullman'. Note the vintage Pullman brake vehicle which is formed immediately behind the locomotive, while the rest of the carriages that are visible are more modern Metro-Cammell Pullmans constructed in the early 1960s. No. D9017 was built at English Electric Co., Vulcan Foundry, Lancashire, and entered traffic at Gateshead in November 1961. It was named in October 1963 and was included in the final batch of withdrawals of these legendary machines, which occurred in December 1981. A number have survived into preservation, but No. D9017 was not so fortunate. It was reduced to scrap at Doncaster Works in January 1983: what a sad end to such a splendid locomotive. *Hugh Ballantyne*

No. D9017 is seen again, this time approaching
Finsbury Park at the head of the 2.00pm King's
Cross to Aberdeen on 9th December 1973. By this
time it had been repainted in the BR corporate
blue colour. In this picture, though, the livery of
the locomotive is purely academic, because the
brilliant low winter sunshine has given the
train – which is beautifully framed by the
signal gantry – an incredible gold-plated appearance.
Chris Gammell

An up empty train of long-distance coaches approaches Harringay station behind Brush Type 2 No. D5586 on 14th May 1960. In those days the rolling stock which had formed trains into King's Cross was often taken out to the carriage sidings at Hornsey or Ferme Park for servicing, and consequently there was a considerable number of empty stock movements which found employment for a small army of steam tank engines. By the time of this picture however, steam traction was obviously not in sole charge of these duties, No. D5586 being one of several diesel locomotives of this type based at Finsbury Park by that time. No. D5586 was a mere three months old when this portrait was taken and became No. 31 168 under the TOPS renumbering scheme of the mid-1970s. It was retired in December 1991 after over thirty years' service. *Frank Hornby*

An unidentified 'Deltic' 3,300hp Type 5 locomotive is depicted approaching Wood Green station in September 1961. Judging by its absolutely immaculate appearance – even the bogies are remarkably clean – the locomotive had presumably only been in traffic a few days at the time of this picture, which may give a clue to its identity. It is possibly No. D9012 *Crepello* which entered service during September 1961, certainly the size of its nameplate seems right for that machine, but who knows? BR may have been investing in new traction at this time, but most of the other railway equipment visible is definitely from the steam age. Note the jointed track, old-fashioned semaphore signalling and the third coach in the train which is a Thompson carriage of pre-nationalisation design. The next vehicle appears to be an even older Gresley restaurant car. Let us hope the passengers did not find them too bouncy as the 'Deltic' was whisking them along at 100mph! The first production series 'Deltic' to arrive at Doncaster Works from the builders was No. D9001 (later named *St Paddy*) which appeared on 23rd February 1961. No. D9000 (later named *Royal Scots Grey*) arrived five days later and was immediately involved in a shunting mishap, which caused it to be sidelined for a few days. Both locomotives were put to work on acceptance trials between Doncaster and Peterborough hauling 14 coaches, and their capabilities were apparent right from the start, No. D9001 touching 100mph down Stoke bank on its second outing. No. D9001 was delivered to Finsbury Park depot on 6th March and later the same day worked to Doncaster and back on parcels trains. The following day it powered the 8.25am King's Cross to Doncaster train, but unfortunately this trip was marred by its failure at Retford with train heating problems. The introduction of the 'Deltics' revolutionised services on the East Coast Main Line and resulted in an almost total recast of schedules from the start of the winter 1961 timetable, with 29 trains booked for mile-a-minute running compared to a paltry six in the previous winter timetable. For example, 'The West Riding' express from King's Cross to Leeds/Bradford was dramatically accelerated, the journey time being reduced by as much as 44min. This train was booked to cover the 106½ miles from Hitchin to Retford in 89 minutes start to stop, at an average speed of 71.8mph. *John Snell*

The prototype Brush 2,800hp Co-Co diesel-electric locomotive, No. D0280 *Falcon* rolls the up 'Sheffield Pullman' through Oakleigh Park in June 1962. This 115-ton locomotive was powered by two pressure-charged and inter-cooled Bristol Siddeley/Maybach engines each producing 1,400hp at 1,500rpm. The engine used in *Falcon* was basically similar to the MD 650 type fitted to the WR's 'Warship' locomotives. When *Falcon* first appeared for trials on BR tracks it created quite a stir due to its lime green livery, which was offset by panels of light brown on the bodywork and orange buffer beams. Its name was enclosed in a falcon silhouette on the bodyside, though this was later replaced by a proper nameplate. No. D0280 was initially based at Finsbury Park, where it was first spotted on 13th October 1961, and its initial reported duties were on King's Cross to Cambridge trains. On October 18th it worked a King's Cross to Hull train as far as Doncaster, returning on an afternoon working as diagrammed. It was later transferred to the WR where it was subjected to comprehensive testing on level track and on steep gradients to evaluate its power unit performance. On level track it reportedly attained a speed of 75mph hauling 600 tons (18 coaches). *Falcon* did particularly well during trials on inclines and on one occasion smoothly started a 638-ton train on the 1 in 37 Lickey incline. By mid-1962 *Falcon* had returned to the ER and was based at Darnall shed (Sheffield) for working the 'Master Cutler' Pullman service to and from London. These duties continued until late 1963 when *Falcon* was returned to Brush Traction for overhaul. It re-emerged painted in Brunswick green livery with small yellow warning panels and saw service alongside 'Westerns' on the Paddington to Bristol run for a time. In 1970 BR purchased the locomotive from Brush at its scrap value and in January 1971 No. D0280 entered Swindon Works for an overhaul, emerging in standard BR blue with full yellow ends as No. 1200. Most of its remaining life was spent at Newport Ebbw Junction shed where it was employed on freight workings, a far cry indeed from the more glamorous 'Master Cutler'. *Falcon* was withdrawn in October 1975 and subsequently sold to Cashmores of Newport, who scrapped the locomotive in March 1976. *A.G. Forsyth/Colour-Rail*

There is no doubt that of all the early prototype diesel locomotives produced by outside manufacturers, the immensely powerful 'Deltic' had the greatest impact. It was constructed at English Electric's Dick Kerr Works, Preston, the frames being laid in early 1955. This Co-Co locomotive was equipped with two Napier & Son type D18–25 engines, each developing 1,650hp, which powered six English Electric traction motors. The 106-ton machine at first had a designated top speed of 90mph, but this was later increased to 105mph. The 'Deltic' was painted in a striking powder blue livery with aluminium mouldings. It was also decorated with cream nose end 'speed whiskers' which BR also, somewhat misguidedly, applied to dmus which hardly merited them! The 'Deltic' was fitted with a headlight, presumably with overseas sales in mind, but this was never used on BR. Strangely, it never carried a number, the original plan to number it DP1 (Diesel Prototype 1) having been abandoned. The 'Deltic's first revenue-earning duties started in December 1955 when it was based at Edge Hill shed, Liverpool, for London services. In early 1959 it was moved to Hornsey shed for possible use on the East Coast Main Line, but spent the first six months of that year on clearance or performance tests on that route; some of the latter included

hauling heavy mineral trains! From July 1959 'Deltic' became a regular performer on East Coast passenger turns where it worked alongside English Electric Type 4s and Gresley Class A4 Pacifics! In March 1961, after covering a creditable 450,000 miles in BR service, a serious engine failure befell 'Deltic', just at the time when the production series machines were becoming available, and it was unceremoniously removed to English Electric's Vulcan Foundry Works. In 1963 'Deltic' was presented to the Science Museum, London, but has since been moved to the National Railway Museum at York, where it remains at the time of writing. The 'Deltic' is seen emerging from Hadley Wood tunnel with an up train in August 1960. *D. Trevor Rowe/Colour-Rail*

'Nice diesel, it's a pity about the coaches', might be the reaction of the average commuter to this picture of Brush 1,365hp Type 2 A1A-A1A No. D5679 leaving Hadley Wood station with a down rush-hour train on the evening of 9th May 1963. Certainly the two wooden-bodied Gresley-designed 'Quad-Art' sets forming the train, which dated from the 1920s, were from a different age compared to the locomotive hauling them, which was just over two years old when this scene was recorded. Most King's Cross suburban services had been taken over by dmus in the late 1950s, so presumably only a few locomotive-hauled rush-hour trains remained. The ancient 'Quad-Art' sets were notoriously uncomfortable, due to the cramped conditions in each compartment, and were later replaced by BR Standard non-corridor coaches which offered slightly more space. This location, which provided a most pleasant, unobstructed view of the line and attractive station beyond, has long been a favourite with railway photographers, and many photographic masterpieces must have been taken there over the years. *Roy Hobbs*

A pair of Southern Region BRCW Type 3s on the East Coast Main Line sometime in 1962! Two unidentified 'Cromptons' head towards London near Ganwick with a cement train, presumably the Uddingston (near Edinburgh) to Cliffe (Kent) return working which was booked for SR Type 3 motive power at that time. Locomotives of this class started operation on this train in about December 1961 and were generally diagrammed to work as far as York, although they reportedly strayed considerably further north on occasions. The first 'Crompton' to venture north along the East Coast route, however, is understood to have been No. D6504 which underwent trials with electrically-heated coaching stock between King's Cross and Edinburgh in February 1961. It is unlikely that these tests had any connection with the later introduction of these machines on the cement trains. SR BRCW Type 3s could often be seen working freight on 'foreign' regions during the 1960s, because other regular diagrams took them to Bromford Bridge, near Birmingham, on oil trains from Fawley. Later in their careers these versatile Type 3s ranged far and wide, and could regularly be observed on Cardiff to Crewe and Exeter to Paignton passenger services, in addition to their wide variety of passenger and freight turns on the Southern Region. *John Snell*

A Cravens-built two-car dmu is illustrated forming an up passenger working, presumably destined for King's Cross, near Brookmans Park on 28th February 1959. The 'blue haze' fumes are the result of a lineside fire. This series of 48 units was introduced in 1958 and consisted of a Driving Trailer Composite with Lavatory vehicle (DTCL), nearest to the camera, and a Driving Motor Brake Second (DMBS) coach. The unit was powered by two AEC 150hp engines and the DTCL carriage weighed 24 tons, while the DMBS was six tons heavier. The former vehicle offered seating for 12 first class passengers and 51 in the second class, while the other coach had 52 second class seats. Note the rather pointless 'speed whiskers' which were painted on the front ends of dmus before the advent of yellow warning panels. In the author's opinion, most diesel units produced under the BR modernisation programme of the 1950s offered spartan seating accommodation, vibrated excessively and were often extremely rough-riding at speeds in excess of 25 mph! In the summer they could be unbearably hot, but during the winter months passengers were frequently frozen due to the tendency of the heating system to shut down just when it was most needed. One wonders if BR ever got even with the designers of these contraptions! *Trevor Owen*

English Electric Type 4 1Co-Co1 No. D206 was only seven months old when photographed near Brookmans Park, hauling a train from Newcastle-upon-Tyne, on a misty 28th February 1959, the same day that the previous shot was taken. The permanent way department have added to the poor visibility by burning lineside vegetation, or perhaps the conflagration had been started by sparks from a passing steam train. Clearly there had been a long, dry spell of weather during the weeks before this picture was taken, which is unusual for that time of year. Following its release to traffic No. D206 was allocated to Hornsey shed and later became a resident of another London depot, Stratford, from where it undertook duties on trains from Liverpool Street to Norwich. Like many of these machines, it ended its days in the north of England, being based at Healey Mills principally for use on coal trains. No. D206 (which became No. 40 006 under the TOPS renumbering system) was withdrawn in March 1983 and met its end at Crewe Works in August 1984. *Trevor Owen/Colour-Rail*

The first Birmingham Railway Carriage & Wagon Co. Type 2 1,160hp Bo-Bo locomotive, 20 of which (Nos D5300–19) had been ordered by the BTC under the modernisation programme, arrived at Hornsey depot in July 1958 for use on suburban and semi-fast passenger duties from King's Cross. Delivery of Hornsey's entire complement had been completed by March 1959. These engines, however, were destined to have a very brief career in the London area. A further batch had been ordered by the BTC and it was decided to allocate these 27 locomotives to the Scottish Region. Subsequently there was a change of policy aimed at concentrating locomotive types in specific areas to ease maintenance problems, and it was decreed that all of the Eastern Region's BRCW Type 2s in the London area were to be transferred to Scotland and replaced by new Brush Type 2s as they became available. So, on 12th April 1960, the first pair of BRCW locomotives, Nos D5300/1, left Hornsey for Doncaster on the first leg of their journey to Scotland. They were taken by a local crew, who returned from Doncaster with Brush Type 2s Nos D5602/3. This arrangement continued for some months until all of the locomotives had been transferred. Here, No. D5311, which was just a few weeks old at the time of the picture, is seen near Brookmans Park on 28th February 1959 powering an up suburban passenger train. *Trevor Owen/Colour-Rail*

THE WIDENED LINES

Home-going commuters are seen waiting on the platform at Farringdon as Brush Type 2 No. 31 221 enters the station at the head of the 5.20pm Moorgate to Hatfield train on 31st July 1974. The train is travelling over the Widened Lines, the Metropolitan Railway's City Extension from King's Cross to Moorgate. The formation comprises of the relatively short-lived BR Standard non-gangwayed coaches, many of which ended their days on trains such as this, most just forming one morning and one evening peak-hour train, five days a week. At least travel in this stock was to be preferred to a rattling diesel unit! Today, there is no direct service from Farringdon to Hatfield, but passengers from Moorgate still have a service via Drayton Park. *Chris Evans*

The Railway Correspondence & Travel Society ran their first 'East London Rail Tour' in 1951, using steam power, of course, and traversing some interesting, little-known lines in that part of the Capital. At that time the only diesel motive power in east London was used for shunting and new classes of steam engines were being delivered for main line operation. But, by the time the society came to operate their 'East London Rail Tour No. 3' on 6th October 1962, this picture had changed completely and its hopes of using steam power for this tour had been dashed when, on 16th September, the last steam locomotives on the Great Eastern Line were withdrawn from service. So, no doubt to the intense disappointment of participants, a Bo-Bo 800hp Type 1 diesel was provided instead of the hoped-for steam locomotive, dozens of which were, tantalisingly, lying out of use at Stratford shed. The locomotive selected to haul the train was No. D8236, a British Thomson-Houston Co. product built in late 1960, which was one of a class totalling 44 examples. This machine is depicted at Liverpool Street prior to departure to North Woolwich, the train's first stop. Later in the day the train visited the Buntingford branch. Little did the participants know it at the time but, mainly due to the decline in cross-London freight traffic on which they were employed, this class was destined to have a very short working life. The last member was withdrawn in 1971, so this shot is of considerable historical interest. *John Edgington*

THE GREAT EASTERN LINE

A steam age diesel locomotive or a diesel age steam locomotive? Many of the diesels featured in this book worked side by side with steam engines for some years before the latter were eventually phased out. In this shot an apparently brand new, unidentified English Electric Type 3 Co-Co rubs shoulders with Great Eastern Railway J69 Class 0-6-0T No 68619 at Liverpool Street station in 1961. The J69 dated from the turn of the century and was kept in immaculate, highly polished condition by Stratford shed for use as the Liverpool Street pilot engine. *T. Linfoot/C. Gammell collection*

In this illustration, one of the oldest shots of a main line diesel locomotive in action in this album, a Brush A1A-A1A 1,250hp Type 2 locomotive, No. D5516, is seen arriving at Liverpool Street with the 11.48am train from Ely on 2nd October 1958. The train had just emerged into daylight after threading the smoky and cavernous cutting in which the railway is confined for most of the way from Bethnal Green station. The viaduct behind the train carried the line from Dalston Junction into Broad Street station. No. D5516 had only been in traffic for a few weeks when this portrait was taken, as evidenced here by its immaculate appearance. In 1974 it was allocated the TOPS number 31 016, but two years afterwards was declared to be 'non standard' and was withdrawn, together with other sister engines amongst the batch of 20 of these 'pilot scheme' locomotives built in the early days of the BR modernisation plan. No. 31 016 met its fate at Doncaster Works in December 1976. *R.C. Riley*

Trains from Liverpool Street face a difficult start which involves a short, but severe, 1 in 70 climb as far as Bethnal Green. Steam enginemen with a 'cold' locomotive probably dreaded the initial mile or so of the run from Liverpool Street, but the crew of English Electric Type 4 2,000hp 1Co-Co1 No. D205, seen here approaching Bethnal Green with the 12.30pm London to Norwich express on 28th February 1959, were no doubt grateful to sit back and let the locomotive take the strain. The former GER main line from Liverpool Street to Norwich was the first to benefit from the introduction of these Type 4 locomotives, the first of which made its debut on the route on 18th March 1958. Six of these machines (Nos D200 to D205) were subsequently allocated to Stratford depot for the Norwich services and were doubtless kept in spotless external condition, which was a hallmark of Stratford shed. No. D205 finished its career based at Healey Mills for hauling freight trains and was unfortunate enough to be one of the first of the class to be condemned, an event which occurred in January 1976. It was broken-up at Crewe Works early in the following year. *R.C. Riley*

Photographed on the same day as the previous picture, Brush Type 2 1,250hp A1A-A1A No. D5514 nears the end of the climb from Liverpool Street with the 12.10pm express to King's Lynn. This train conveyed, in addition to a buffet car, through carriages to Hunstanton, a location which lost its rail connection in the Beeching economies of the 1960s. The vehicle immediately behind the locomotive is an *ex*-LNER Thompson-designed coach which appears to have a very large guard's van, in contrast to many trains today which do not have one at all! Many of the locomotives of this type which were built slightly later than No. D5514 had long, albeit unremarkable, working lives, but this machine was deemed to be non-standard and became an early withdrawal casualty in November 1976. *R.C. Riley*

Unsurprisingly, most of the illustrations in this album are from the era of the late 1950s and early 1960s when most BR diesel locomotives classes bore a distinctive, and sometimes quite colourful, livery. Regrettably the change of policy in favour of the corporate livery in the mid-1960s heralded what was surely one of the dullest and most uninspiring periods on Britain's railways when, regardless of its shape or size, every locomotive (and most coaches) was painted in one of the drabbest shades of blue ever seen! Needless to say the paint rapidly faded and did not withstand the weather as well as the more durable and attractive BR green. It may have been a bonanza period for the paint manufacturers, but camera film processors probably saw their takings plummet! Here, an English Electric Type 3, No. 6964, passes Stratford in charge of an unidentified down express on 28th August 1971. In addition to its awful blue paintwork, the locomotive is further disfigured by a curious, streaky grey 'stripe' on its lower bodyside panels, presumably a deposit of cleaning fluid which has not been washed off. Oh dear! *Frank Hornby*

Looking extremely smart with its shiny new paintwork, North British 1,100hp Type 2 Bo-Bo No. D6114 poses at Stratford shed on 7th June 1959. This locomotive had a MAN L12V/18/21S engine which powered four GEC traction motors. Ten of these machines were ordered by the BTC as part of the pilot scheme for traction modernisation and the first one rolled off the company's production line at Queen's Park Works, Glasgow, in 1958. After testing in Scotland, the locomotives started to arrive at Hornsey depot for service on GN suburban services. The class could hardly be described as a glittering success, however, and almost from the start they were the source of many headaches for operating and maintenance staff. During acceptance trials in April 1959 it is recorded that No. D6107 failed on the East Coast main line, causing considerable disruption to traffic, and the unreliability of other members of the class became apparent even before they entered service. Alas, BR made the crucial mistake of ordering further locomotives, some of which were subsequently employed in East Anglia, before the initial batch had been fully evaluated, and by early 1960 major technical difficulties had become apparent. BR then decided to move the entire Eastern Region allocation to Scotland, apparently as part of a policy of concentrating locomotive types in one area for maintenance purposes. This decision also had the advantage that these ill-fated and unpredictable locomotives would be operating close to the manufacturer's works where remedial action could be undertaken when the need arose. Hornsey shed's allocation was transferred north in April 1960, the locomotives moving to Scotland in pairs, presumably just in case one broke down on the way! The machines based in East Anglia followed in August and September and it is recorded that No. D6114 was in the final group of engines to leave the ER, on 13th September. Despite the class's appalling reliability 57 examples were built, the last entering traffic in December 1960 in Scotland. The class continued to perform erratically and in early 1963 one locomotive was re-engined with a 1,350hp Paxman 'Ventura' power unit, which proved more reliable than the locomotive's MAN engine. A further 19 members of the class were later fitted with this type of engine. Some of the unmodified locomotives spent long periods stored out of use, and many were withdrawn in late 1967. Further substantial withdrawals followed in 1968, leaving the re-engined locomotives to soldier on until they, too, were taken out of service in 1971. This class was undoubtedly an unmitigated disaster, so it is, perhaps, fortunate that no examples were preserved to remind past and future taxpayers of that fact! *R.C. Riley*

Type 1 Bo-Bo locomotive No. D8406, seen here at Stratford on 7th June 1959, was one of a class of ten machines ordered from NBL under the BR modernisation plan 'pilot scheme' in 1956. These locomotives were equipped with an 800hp Paxman engine and delivery to Stratford shed commenced in May 1958 with the final example entering service in September of that year. Unfortunately, the locomotives did not live up to expectations and problems were immediately experienced with their power units which frequently seized up. Additionally, the cylinder heads repeatedly failed and the unreliable non-standard control equipment was also a source of concern. The locomotives were concentrated at Stratford throughout their lives, being used on light cross-London freights in between regular visits to Stratford Works for attention. The decline in this sort of traffic in the late 1960s, coupled with their poor operating history led to the inescapable conclusion that the locomotives would always be a liability and it would be prudent to eliminate the class. The complete class was withdrawn in 1968 and all the locomotives scrapped, an event which brought to a close another embarrassing chapter in the history of the modernisation plan. *R.C. Riley*

Looking somewhat dwarfed by the lofty and impressive Abbey Mills Junction signal box which towers above it, British Thomson-Houston Co. 800hp Bo-Bo No. D8229 is depicted working a freight train near Stratford on 31st March 1962. This was another class introduced under the modernisation programme – the first member appeared in November 1957 – which was not entirely successful, and many were taken out of service in the late 1960s, their withdrawal being hastened by a contraction in the freight business. Other representatives of the type lingered until early 1971. After the class ceased line work, four locomotives were redeployed as carriage heating units and one of these, No. D8233 (latterly ADB 968001), was later purchased privately for preservation. *R.C. Riley*

A most interesting interior view, taken in October 1959, of the diesel shop at Stratford Works showing the prototype 'Deltic' receiving attention. It is recorded that this locomotive was still undergoing repair on 1st January 1960, so perhaps it needed fairly extensive attention, or maybe it was 'stopped' awaiting the arrival of a vital spare part. The shortage of spares particularly affected small classes: in this case the class consisted of one locomotive! At the time of this photograph, Stratford Works was still repairing steam locomotives, but a large proportion of the steam engines arriving at the works were for cutting-up. Diesel work was rapidly increasing, partly due to the alarmingly high failure rate of many of the new diesel types. At the beginning of 1960, in addition to the 'Deltic', the diesel shop was attending to a variety of diesel shunters, English Electric and North British Type 1s, BR/Sulzer and Brush Type 2s, and one of the failure-prone 'Baby Deltics', which was doubtless present for an engine change. All of these classes would be regarded as museum pieces today. *A. Morris/Colour-Rail*

In 1956 English Electric constructed two prototype 500hp 0–6–0 diesel shunters at Vulcan Foundry, Newton-le-Willows, Lancashire. They were specifically designed for freight transfer work between goods and marshalling yards, and were faster and more powerful than the standard 350hp shunters being introduced in large numbers at that time. No. D226 had electric transmission, while No. D227 was fitted with hydraulic transmission, and extensive trials, which commenced in July 1957, were arranged on BR to compare the two types and carry out a general evaluation. During the course of the trials it was clearly demonstrated that the former was the superior system. It also became clear, however, that the locomotives were not sufficiently powerful for the type of work for which they had been designed, these duties being better handled by machines of 1,000hp or more. In order to avoid a duplication of running numbers with the English Electric Type 4s, which were numbered in the D200 series, the locomotives were renumbered D0226 and D0227 in August 1959. The latter was, however, withdrawn during September 1959 and later scrapped, but its sister engine survived on BR metals until October 1960. No. D0226 is known to have worked at a wide variety of locations during its period on loan to BR, including Liverpool, Doncaster, Bristol and Swindon in addition to Stratford, where both machines were photographed on 11th July 1959. No. D0226 was stored at its birthplace for six years following the end of its BR tests, and was sometimes used for shunting. In March 1966 it was despatched on permanent loan to the Keighley & Worth Valley Railway, in West Yorkshire, where it was used on works trains. On very rare occasions it has been known to deputise at short notice for a steam locomotive on a passenger train. No. D0226 was later named *Vulcan* by the society. *T.B. Owen/Colour-Rail*

The diminutive locomotive (undoubtedly the most impressive in this album!) seen in this picture is a Ruston & Hornsby 0-4-0 165hp diesel mechanical shunter, which was built in 1956. It weighed a mere 28 tons and had wheels of 3′4″ diameter. This locomotive was generally typical of a range of small diesel shunters which was produced in the mid-1950s by builders such as Andrew Barclay, Hunslet and Hudswell-Clarke. No. D2958 was originally numbered 11508 and was one of two machines constructed to this design for BR use. It began life at Immingham, but was withdrawn from service at Stratford in January 1968. It was photographed at the latter location on 5th November 1961. After its withdrawal No. D2958 was sold by BR for industrial use and survived until late 1984. *Paul Leavens*

In early 1960 two Brush Type 2s – Nos D5578 and D5579 – were experimentally painted in non-standard liveries, apparently to enable proposed new locomotive freight liveries to be assessed. The former was painted in duck-egg blue, while the latter machine was turned out in golden ochre. Neither locomotive lasted very long in its new colours and both were repainted in standard BR green during their first works repair, so it can be assumed that these liveries did not withstand everyday service particularly well. Here, No. D5579 presents a cheerful sight at Stratford depot in 1960. This locomotive later became No. 31 161 in the TOPS renumbering scheme and was subsequently fitted with electric train heating, becoming No. 31 400. It was withdrawn in October 1991 and was dismantled for scrap at Booth Roe Metals Ltd, Rotherham, in August 1993. *Colour-Rail*

English Electric Type 3 Co-Co No. 6832 eases an oil tank train across the maze of tracks at the approach to Stratford Station on 28th April 1971. This sturdy class has really stood the test of time and forty years after its introduction, in December 1960, it can still be seen (at the time of writing) in small numbers on a variety of work across Great Britain, although most are now confined to departmental duties. During the year 2000 the class also retained a few passenger diagrams, mainly along the North Wales coast, and in Scotland, and had become a firm favourite amongst diesel haulage enthusiasts as a result of the locomotives' distinctive exhaust sound. *Frank Hornby*

The shadows are lengthening as the up 'Bournemouth Belle' passes through Vauxhall station behind Brush Type 4 No. D1922 on the evening of Friday 7th July 1967, just two days prior to the end of steam on the Southern Region. The 'Belle' was by this time rostered for a Brush Type 4 in each direction, but had produced steam traction on four occasions during the last week of steam, so it is likely that the photographer was hoping for a steam engine but, alas, on this occasion he was disappointed. In late 1966 the SR had six Brush Type 4s drafted in from the Western Region ostensibly to assist the run-down steam fleet. For obvious reasons these locomotives were given uncomplimentary names by the steam fans and possibly also by the operating staff, because the diesels proved to be most unreliable and were often substituted by steam motive power, the reverse of what was intended! *R.C. Riley*

SOUTHERN REGION – SOUTH WESTERN DIVISION

A sad moment in history as the empty stock of the 'Bournemouth Belle' leaves Clapham Yard for the last time on 9th July 1967. Motive power is provided by BRCW Type 3 Bo-Bo No. D6515. The 'Belle' ceased operation from the following day when the Bournemouth electrification scheme was brought fully into use and modern traction replaced steam, which was completely eliminated from the Southern Region. The 'Bournemouth Belle' had run continuously, apart from a wartime interruption, since 1931 and it had been expected that this famous train would go out on a high note with a gleaming Bulleid Pacific at its head. Predictably, perhaps, the SR management of the day dashed such optimistic hopes when they decreed that the final workings must be diesel-hauled. The task of hauling the last workings of the 'Belle' fell to Brush Type 4 No. D1924. *John Hayward*

Another picture taken on the evening of 7th July 1967, the last weekday of steam operation on the SR. The 6.22pm Waterloo to Bournemouth train passes through Clapham cutting, just south of Clapham Junction station, with a 'Crompton', No. D6538, in charge. The photographer was probably hoping that this train would be steam hauled, as booked, but this BRCW Type 3, which had obviously been released recently from Eastleigh Works following conversion to push-pull operation, appeared instead. The train is formed of a selection of Bulleid and BR Standard coaches in green livery, in contrast to the locomotive in shiny blue and yellow. *Chris Gammell*

Photographed on the bright and clear day of 25th February 1967, a rather dirty Brush Type 4, No. D1925, gathers speed as it passes Raynes Park with an unspecified Waterloo to Bournemouth train. The young enthusiast standing on the platform with his camera appears to be completely unmoved. By this time there was a total of six of these locomotives, Nos D1921–26, available on the SR for use on the South Western Division. All came from the Western Region, the first to arrive being No. D1923 which was officially transferred to Eastleigh in September 1966 for crew training purposes. This was followed by Nos D1921/22 in October and Nos D1924/5/6 in December. These machines were put to work on the heaviest expresses and by January 1967 had officially replaced steam traction on six weekday trains from Waterloo and, of course, their corresponding return workings. *Frank Hornby*

A train from Waterloo to Exeter is illustrated approaching Esher behind 'Warship' Class No. D869 *Zest* in May 1966. Note that although the WR supplied the motive power for these trains SR coaching stock was still being used, and in this case most of the vehicles visible are of Bulleid design. The 'Warship' locomotives, and especially those constructed by the North British Locomotive Company, were not one of the most reliable types to be built under the BR modernisation plan. In addition they had hydraulic transmission, which was non-standard, and these factors made them candidates for early elimination. They were replaced on these trains by SR Type 3s in the early 1970s. *Geoff Rixon*

Another view at Esher, but this time looking west towards the station. The train in this study is an unidentified London-bound express with BRCW Type 3 No. D6507 in charge, which had not yet been disfigured by a yellow warning panel. Once again, Bulleid-designed rolling stock is to the fore, the carriage formed immediately behind the engine also being a BRCW product, but from a somewhat earlier period. This picture was taken in June 1966. *Geoff Rixon*

This scene at Byfleet Junction shows BRCW Type 3 Bo-Bo No. D6509 passing with a down Bournemouth train on a sunny morning in February 1967. The down line from Addlestone, which in days gone by was used by many freight trains from Feltham yard, can be seen on the right. The corresponding up line to Addlestone is not visible in the shot. Note that the train is made up of two TC units in corporate blue livery: the classification 'TC' indicated a trailer corridor unit. These three and four-coach units, which were unpowered, were designed to work in multiple with the high-powered 4-REP units on the Waterloo to Bournemouth line. The TCs were extremely versatile and could be hauled or propelled by a BRCW Type 3 diesel or electro-diesel locomotive. At the time of this picture, the SR operating authorities were anxious to reduce steam activity to a minimum and steam-hauled services were being replaced by a combination of a BRCW Type 3 plus TC sets, as seen here. *Geoff Rixon*

The Southern Region's premier long-distance route was undoubtedly that from Waterloo to the West of England, which was well known for its fast schedules and multi-portioned trains serving the holiday resorts of Devon and Cornwall. Perhaps the most famous train on this line was the celebrated 'Atlantic Coast Express' which first ran in 1928 and was given the SR's first mile-a-minute schedule in 1952. In 1963, however, the Western Region obtained control of this legendary route, quickly downgrading it in status and then carrying out a draconian rationalisation which reduced long stretches to single track. The last weekday 'Atlantic Coast Express' ran on 4th September 1964 and three days later the WR introduced a semi-fast diesel-hauled service between Waterloo and Exeter only, and all through carriages to the coastal resorts, which had been such an invaluable facility on this route, were withdrawn. The WR employed moderately-powered Type 4 'Warship' Class B-B locomotives on the new service, one of which, No. D822 *Hercules* is depicted speeding through Byfleet & New Haw station with a London-bound train in February 1967. *Geoff Rixon*

SOUTHERN REGION – CENTRAL DIVISION

In the 1970s there was still a fair volume of cross-London freight traffic and, south of the River Thames, Norwood Yard was a focus of much of this activity. Here, the 1.12pm mixed freight working from Norwood Yard to Acton is illustrated heading through Balham on the slow line behind Brush Type 4 No. 1739, which still retained two-tone green livery. It would have been routed via the West London Line from which it would have diverged at Mitre Bridge Junction to reach Acton Yard. This portrait was taken on 3rd April 1973. *Chris Evans*

The 1.12pm Norwood yard to Acton freight is seen again, this time near Norbury on 12th February 1974, with more interesting motive power in the shape of 'Western' Class diesel hydraulic locomotive No. D1072 *Western Glory* in charge. By this date the 'Westerns' had already been reduced in strength by a number of withdrawals which continued steadily until the last of the class was taken out of traffic in early 1977. No. D1072, a Crewe product dating from November 1963, lasted until almost the very end of the class, being withdrawn in November 1976. At the date of this picture Beyer Peacock (Hymek) Type 3 B-Bs could also be seen on this working in addition to Brush Type 4s and 'Westerns'. *Chris Evans*

The 12.09pm Victoria to East Grinstead train, led by 3D unit No. 1310 speeds through Thornton Heath station on 14th May 1974. The rear unit appears to be a 3H 'Hampshire' type. The 3D units were introduced in 1962, the first one being delivered to St Leonards depot on 4th April with the remainder being progressively introduced during the following months, the full complement being in traffic by September. At first these units were known as the 'East Sussex' stock, but later they were generally referred to as 'Oxted' units because most of their duties were on that route. The middle vehicles were rather unusual, consisting of a three bay second class saloon, four first class compartments, a lavatory and a further two bay second class saloon, all of which were connected by a side corridor. This stock had a narrow Restriction 1 body profile to enable it to pass through Grove tunnel between Tunbridge Wells West and Central stations. The 'Oxted' units had a deserved reputation for rough riding at speed and it was no doubt to the relief of Oxted Line travellers when the bulk of the units were scrapped following electrification of the East Grinstead route in 1987. A few 'Oxted' type vehicles survive at the time of writing on the Hastings to Ashford 'Marshlink' line. *Chris Evans*

On 20th April 1975 the South Eastern Division's main line was completely closed by engineering works at Sevenoaks and consequently a number of Charing Cross to Hastings trains were diverted to run via the Brighton Line. In this shot, Hastings Line demu No. 1012 has just taken the Quarry Line at Coulsdon North with the 11.40am *ex*-Charing Cross and is seen rattling across the points where the Redhill route diverges. The scene from this viewpoint has altered considerably since this picture was taken, perhaps the most significant change being the closure of Coulsdon North station, the tracks and platforms of which are just visible on the extreme left. It is amazing to think that for generations Coulsdon was served by no fewer than three stations situated within a quarter of a mile of each other! An attractive feature of this shot is Coulsdon North signal box, but this has also disappeared, in this case a victim of the resignalling of the Brighton Line which was completed in 1985. *Chris Evans*

Facing page The use of a picture of an SR electro-diesel in this album is slightly controversial, perhaps, but there can be no doubt that it qualifies for inclusion. Here, in a rare shot of a Civil Engineer's Department ballast train, No. 73 103 is depicted approaching Honor Oak Park with a New Cross Gate to Norwood Yard working on 21st October 1974. Note the brilliant autumn colours of the lineside trees. The bridge in the background is a roadbridge which is partially hiding another bridge carrying the South Eastern's Catford loop across the line. *Chris Gammell*

Despite the overcast conditions, spotlessly clean Brush Type 2 No. 5518 still manages to make an eye-catching sight at the head of the Royal Train conveying HM the Queen and HRH the Duke of Edinburgh to Tattenham Corner on Derby Day, 4th June 1969. The train was photographed near Chipstead. The Royal saloon is the second vehicle from the engine, this being marshalled in front of a Metro-Cammell Pullman car in BR corporate blue and grey livery. The other two coaches appear to be BR Standard Mk 1 BSKs. No. 5518, which was one of the first batch of these locomotives, would have originally been fitted with headcode discs, not a four character route indicator as seen here. Presumably this machine had suffered collision damage at some stage during its career and the opportunity had been taken to fit a headcode panel. The traditional Royal Train from Victoria to Tattenham Corner had been steam-hauled for many years, but steam traction bowed out in 1964. The Bulleid electric locomotives took over in 1965, but did not last long, the last of the class being withdrawn in late 1968. Consequently, this left the SR without any locomotives fitted with a steam heating boiler, so the Eastern Region solved the problem by providing Stratford shed's No. 5518. This was the first time the Derby Day 'Royal' was diesel hauled. *John Scrace*

A fleet of Type 3 locomotives had been ordered by the British Transport Commission in 1957 specifically for use on the SR, but delivery was delayed and the SR filled the gap by borrowing some of the first series of BR/Sulzer Type 2s, which had been earmarked for the LMR. The introduction of these machines was not without problems, however, due to the fact that the first locomotive to be finished, No. D5000, was reportedly found to be much heavier than had been anticipated. This prompted the Civil Engineer to impose route restrictions on the class, including stretches of line where the type was to have been used, and modifications were carried out on the locomotives, including the removal of train heating boilers in some cases. Initially, the locomotives were also prohibited from working in multiple, but despite these drawbacks the class was soon noted in service, one of the first reported turns being a Hither Green to Hoo Junction freight train in April 1959. The embargo on the class working in multiple was soon lifted, however, and it started haulage of some continental boat trains from 20th June, Nos D5007/10 being recorded on the 3.42pm SO relief from Victoria to Folkestone Harbour on that date. Here an unidentified pair of these machines is seen near Shortlands, hauling a down continental relief express, during the summer of 1959. *The late Ken Wightman*

Despite the launch of the new BR corporate blue colour scheme in 1965, rolling stock continued to be seen in the old liveries for many years afterwards, and even as late as 1974 a maroon-liveried set of Mk 1 coaches was still active on the LMR, albeit with extremely faded paintwork! The two-tone green livery of this unknown Brush Type 4, seen here approaching St Mary Cray with a down passenger train in 1970, also appears to be the worse for wear, its paintwork being further disfigured by oily deposits on its bodyside.
Ken Smith

A lengthy train bound for the coal terminal at Southfleet passes St Mary Cray Junction behind BR/Sulzer 1Co-Co1 Type 4 No. 108 in September 1971. Note the short-wheelbase four-wheeled wagons which form the train; such vehicles were notoriously prone to derailment at high speeds and were therefore permanently restricted to 45mph. The originating point of this train was probably Toton yard, in the East Midlands coalfield. Unlike certain other classes commonly used north of the River Thames, these machines have never had a high profile on the SR and were probably best known on the 'Southern' for their appearances on the Stirling to Newhaven 'car-sleeper' train in the mid-1960s, apart from freight workings such as this one, which were common at that time. *Ken Smith*

In addition to its extremely dense commuter traffic, the South Eastern Division also had a considerable number of freight flows, principally domestic coal, oil and cement, plus regular cross-channel freight services. Daytime freight services had to be slotted in between the peaks – travellers on a commuter train would not take kindly to being delayed by a slow-moving freight working – so the planning of such workings had to be really precise. Here, a couple of BR/Sulzer Type 2s, with No. 25 131 leading, take an up empty coal train past Swanley in September 1975. By this time the TOPS numbering system was in use and this type was known as Class 25. No. 25 131 is in blue livery, but its unidentified sister engine appears still to be in two-tone green colours, a mere ten years after the change to blue livery began! *Ken Smith*

A most interesting illustration of English Electric Type 1 Bo-Bo No. D8036 at Nunhead with a Poplar Docks to Hither Green sidings freight in April 1961. These locations are only about five miles apart, but it is likely that this train would have been routed via the North London line and Kensington Olympia – a most circuitous and tortuous route. Transfer freight trains such as this have become a thing of the past, following BR's abandonment of wagon-load traffic many years ago in favour of block trains. The old-fashioned, short-wheelbase wagons which form the train have also been consigned to the history books. *Paul Leavens*

In this picture, which was taken later on the same day as the previous photograph, No. D8036 is seen returning home with a train from Hither Green to Bow. This shot was also taken at Nunhead. The line diverging to the right is the Catford loop, while the formation of the Crystal Palace High Level branch is in the foreground. No. D8036 entered traffic in October 1959 and spent some years based at Willesden depot. It must have travelled far and wide during its lifetime, finishing its career in June 1984 at Eastfield shed, Glasgow. *Paul Leavens*

In this further picture taken at Nunhead, BR/Sulzer Type 2 No. D5064 is depicted heading for Hither Green with a train from Brent sidings, also in April 1961. This train would have been routed via the West London line. The location of the photograph is about two hundred yards east of the spot where the previous shot was taken, beyond the junction where the Catford loop diverges. The building which is partially visible on the extreme left of the picture is an electricity sub-station, one of a number which were built to a similar design. The train is traversing the route of the former Nunhead to Greenwich Park branch, which had been dormant for a number of years following its closure in 1917. In 1929, however, a connection was laid from this line to Lewisham station, and a further curve gave access to the London to Tonbridge route, thus enabling cross-London freight trains to reach Hither Green without having to negotiate the heavily congested and tortuous tracks through London Bridge station. Later the section as far as Lewisham was electrified, thereby permitting electric trains to run from Holborn Viaduct to Dartford. *Paul Leavens*

The selection of South Eastern Division photographs which precede this illustration largely feature motive power from other regions and, perhaps, give a slightly unrepresentative picture of everyday working, in which the SR's own BRCW Type 3 (later Class 33) locomotives were very prominent. This shot has, therefore, been included to redress the balance! It shows an unidentified member of the class passing through Hither Green station towards Lewisham with a freight train, apparently a Marinex empties for Cliffe, on 21st September 1975. These extremely versatile machines first arrived on the SR way back in 1960. A large contingent was based at Hither Green shed, which was located just a few hundred yards from where this shot was taken, with the remainder being maintained at Eastleigh depot. The Class 33s stood the all-important test of time magnificently. What better recommendation could there be? *Ken Smith*

Even their best friends would not describe the 'Hastings' demus as handsome. Their narrow, no-frills body profile gave them a rather stark, functional appearance, but at least they fulfilled their purpose, unlike some of the unfortunate and ill-fated locomotive classes featured in this album! In this view unit No. 1037 – one of the small number with a buffet car – dashes down the 1 in 143 gradient from Polhill tunnel with a Charing Cross to Hastings train, which is formed of twelve vehicles. This splendid picture was taken on a glorious June evening in 1975. Two series of these distinctive units were built, the first batch for Phase One of the Hastings Line dieselisation scheme in June 1957, while the second series of units was constructed for Phase Two, which was implemented almost exactly a year later. In later years, the 'Hastings' units became a real headache – and very costly – to maintain due to extensive bodywork corrosion, and it was largely due to the laudable co-operation of the maintenance team at St Leonards depot, and the efforts of Eastleigh Works, that the published timetable continued to operate. In more usual circumstances the operating authorities would have transferred stock from elsewhere to make up any shortfall, but in the case of the Hastings Line that was one option which was definitely not available, due to the narrow tunnels on the route which precluded the use of any other stock. *Ken Smith*

THE WEST LONDON LINE

This vintage scene was photographed in the days before inexpensive continental holidays became popular with the masses and largely replaced the traditional seaside holiday at a British resort. It shows the 12.13pm Ramsgate to Derby Friargate holiday train changing engines on one of the through lines at Kensington Olympia on 22nd August 1959. The train had arrived from the Kent Coast behind a couple of almost brand new BR/Sulzer Type 2s, Nos D5009 and D5003, and these locomotives are about to be uncoupled while 'Black Five' No. 45260, in the background, waits by the platform to take over. At this time a huge number of holiday trains was operated by BR during the summer months, particularly in July and August when children were on holiday from school. This annual exodus placed an enormous burden on the operating authorities as they struggled to provide extra trains to coastal resorts up and down the country. When the late Doctor (later Lord) Beeching took control as the Chairman of BR in 1961 he soon identified these holiday trains – for which a vast pool of little-used rolling stock was retained – as hopelessly uneconomic, and such trains were rapidly phased out. *R.C. Riley*

Photographed against a typical background of West London rooftops, WR 'Warship' Class B–B diesel-hydraulic No. 829 *Magpie* poses in the autumn sunshine at Kensington Olympia on 4th October 1971. Kensington North Main signal box, which presumably controlled the rather fine signal gantry, is prominent on the left of the shot. The 'Warship' had about ten more months of life remaining when this picture was taken, being withdrawn in the following August. It was broken-up at Swindon Works in January 1974. *R.C. Riley*

A busy scene at Kensington Olympia on 6th October 1971 as English Electric 1,750hp Type 3 Co-Co No. 6720 approaches the station with a southbound train of oil tank wagons, while a BR/Sulzer Type 2 Bo-Bo, No. 5215, waits on an adjacent road. In addition, a signal is 'off' for a northbound train. For many years the potential of this station – and the West London line generally – went unrecognised, and it saw little regular passenger traffic. It was probably most famous as the starting point of many 'Motorail' services, and as the destination for a handful of rush-hour trains from Clapham Junction, which were run principally for Post Office staff and did not always appear in the public timetable. Latterly the West London line has seen a resurgence in passenger traffic and now has a regular Brighton to Rugby service and a Clapham Junction to Willesden shuttle, both of which provide a host of travel opportunities. *R.C. Riley*